LOVE
IS ALL
YOU
NEED

LOVE IS ALL YOU NEED

With thanks to Agatha Russell

Summersdale Publishers Ltd
46 West Street
Chichester
West Sussex
PO19 1RP
UK

www.summersdale.com

Printed and bound in the Czech Republic

ISBN: 978-1-84953-870-1

Substantial discounts on bulk quantities of Summersdale books are available to corporations, professional associations and other organisations. For details contact Nicky Douglas by telephone: +44 (0) 1243 756902, fax: +44 (0) 1243 786300 or email: nicky@summersdale.com.

To...

From...

The best thing to
hold on to in life is
each other.

Audrey Hepburn

The more I think it over,
the more I feel that there is
nothing more truly artistic
than to love people.

Vincent van Gogh

Gravitation is not
responsible for people
falling in love.

Albert Einstein

Love that is
not madness
is not love.

Pedro Calderón de la Barca

The important thing is
not the object of love,
but the emotion itself.

Gore Vidal

Who, being loved,
is poor?

Oscar Wilde

Love is too
beautiful to ever
be hidden

We loved with a
love that was more
than love.

Edgar Allan Poe

Love is a human
experience, not a
political statement.

Anne Hathaway

Absence diminishes
small loves and increases
great ones, as the wind
blows out the candle
and fans the bonfire.

François de La Rochefoucauld

If grass can grow
through cement, then
love can find you at
every time in your life.

Cher

Seize the moments of
happiness, love and be loved!
That is the only reality in
the world, all else is folly.

Leo Tolstoy

At the touch of love,
everyone becomes
a poet.

Plato

Eskimos had 52 names
for snow because it
was important to them:
there ought to be as
many for love.

Margaret Atwood

Your fortune is
misfortune if it is
not love.

silent lotus

Yours is the light by which
my spirit's born… you
are my sun, my moon,
and all my stars.

E. E. Cummings

Everything is clearer
when you are in love.

John Lennon

Follow your
heart!

Love is my religion –
I could die for that.
I could die for you.

John Keats

I don't wish to be
everything to everyone,
but I would like to be
something to someone.

Ali Javan

Love rests on no foundation.
It is an endless ocean,
with no beginning or end.

Rumi

There is only one
happiness in life:
to love and be loved.

George Sand

Love is smiling on the
inside and out.

Jennifer Williams

To love is to receive a
glimpse of heaven.

Karen Sunde

What the world really
needs is more love
and less paperwork.

Pearl Bailey

Who would give a law
to lovers? Love is unto
itself a higher law.

Boethius

True love stories
never have endings.

Richard Bach

Love brilliantly, and without regret

Love is the greatest
refreshment in life.

Pablo Picasso

There is no charm equal
to tenderness of heart.

Jane Austen

I am in you and
you in me, mutual
in divine love.

William Blake

I love you without knowing how, or when, or from where. I love you simply, without problems or pride.

Pablo Neruda

Tradition wears a
snowy beard, romance
is always young.

John Greenleaf Whittier

When you fish for love,
bait with your heart,
not your brain.

Mark Twain

Love is composed of a
single soul inhabiting
two bodies.

Aristotle

Love is the law of life.

Mahatma Gandhi

A noble hunger, long unsatisfied, met at last its proper food.

C. S. Lewis on falling in love

Love looks not with eyes,
but with the mind;
And therefore is winged
Cupid painted blind.

William Shakespeare

Love conquers all; let
us, too, yield to love.

Virgil

A caress is better
than a career.

Elisabeth Marbury

Love is a
beautiful dream.

William Sharp

The best part
of me is you

All love is sweet,
given or returned.

Percy Bysshe Shelley

Love is but the discovery of ourselves in others, and the delight in the recognition.

Alexander Smith

A life without love is like
a year without summer.

Swedish proverb

Without love, I should
be spiritless.

François Maynard

Keep love in your heart.
A life without it is like a
sunless garden when
the flowers are dead.

Oscar Wilde

Love is the only
force capable of
transforming an
enemy into a friend.

Martin Luther King Jr

There's nothing more precious in this world than the feeling of being wanted.

Diana Dors

There's no substitute
for a great love who
says, 'No matter what's
wrong with you, you're
welcome at this table.'

Tom Hanks

Two souls are sometimes created together and in love before they're born.

F. Scott Fitzgerald

You come to love not by
finding the perfect person,
but by learning to see an
imperfect person perfectly.

Sam Keen

We love because
it's the only true
adventure.

Nikki Giovanni

Love one another and you
will be happy. It's as simple
and as difficult as that.

Michael Leunig

I love. I have loved.
I will love.

Dodie Smith

Love is a right,
not a wrong

I love you –
I am at rest with you –
I have come home.

Dorothy L. Sayers

All love is original, no
matter how many other
people have loved before.

George Weinberg

If I know what love is,
it is because of you.

Hermann Hesse

Life is the flower for which
love is the honey.

Victor Hugo

Romance is the glamour
which turns the dust
of everyday life into
a golden haze.

Elinor Glyn

Passion is
momentary; love
is enduring.

John Wooden

Things often happen
when you least
expect them to.

Spanish proverb

Looking back, I have this to
regret, that too often when
I loved, I did not say so.

David Grayson

Are we not like two
volumes of one book?

Marceline Desbordes-Valmore

Ah me! Love cannot
be cured by herbs.

Ovid

If I loved you less, I might
be able to talk about it more.

Jane Austen

If music be the food
of love, play on.

William Shakespeare

Love is
beautifully
blind!

Love will draw an
elephant through
a keyhole.

Samuel Richardson

For small creatures
such as we the
vastness is bearable
only through love.

Carl Sagan

I love that feeling of
being in love… of having
butterflies when you wake
up in the morning.

Jennifer Aniston

Love knows no
answer, for it does
not question.

silent lotus

The madness of love
is the greatest of
heaven's blessings.

Plato

You know you're in
love when you can't
fall asleep because
reality is finally better
than your dreams.

Anonymous

When we find someone
whose weirdness is
compatible with ours, we…
fall into mutually satisfying
weirdness – and call it love.

Robert Fulghum

Falling in love
could be achieved
in a single word –
a glance.

Ian McEwan

If you do not love me
I shall not be loved.
If I do not love you
I shall not love.

Samuel Beckett

Love is the
only gold.

Alfred, Lord Tennyson

You are my only love.
You have me completely
in your power.

James Joyce

Thou art to me a
delicious torment.

Ralph Waldo Emerson

Love is most nearly itself
When here and now
cease to matter.

T. S. Eliot

The quarrel of lovers
is the renewal of love.

English proverb

Keep calm and love whoever you want

Where there is
great love there are
always miracles.

Willa Cather

People should fall in love
with their eyes closed.

Andy Warhol

A kiss is a lovely trick
designed by nature to
stop words when speech
becomes unnecessary.

Ingrid Bergman

Love is a canvas
furnished by Nature
and embroidered by
imagination.

Voltaire

Darkness cannot
drive out darkness;
only light can do that.
Hate cannot drive out hate;
only love can do that.

Martin Luther King Jr

Anyone can be
passionate, but it
takes real lovers
to be silly.

Rose Franken

A heart that loves is
always young.

Greek proverb

I love thee – I love thee!
'Tis all that I can say;
It is my vision in the night,
My dreaming in the day.

Thomas Hood

True love begins
when nothing is
looked for in return.

Antoine de Saint-Exupéry

I will make a palace
fit for you and me,
Of green days in forests
and blue days at sea.

Robert Louis Stevenson

May we so love as
never to have occasion
to repent of our love.

Henry David Thoreau

*All love
is equal*

Love does not alter the
beloved, it alters itself.

Søren Kierkegaard

To love is to will the
good of the other.

Thomas Aquinas

True love doesn't come to you; it has to be inside you.

Julia Roberts

So, fall asleep love,
loved by thee.

Robert Browning

There are never
enough 'I love you's.

Lenny Bruce

If you wish to be
loved, love.

Seneca the Younger

In art as in love,
instinct is enough.

Anatole France

Heard melodies are sweet,
but those unheard
are sweeter.

John Keats

Love is everything it's
cracked up to be.

Erica Jong

Each time you love, love as deeply as if it were for ever.

Audre Lorde

My bounty is as
boundless as the sea,
My love as deep; the
more I give to thee,
The more I have, for
both are infinite.

William Shakespeare

All you need is love.
But a little chocolate now
and then doesn't hurt.

Charles M. Schulz

Those who matter
don't mind, and
those who mind
don't matter.

Bernard Baruch

Love is the only sane
and satisfactory answer
to the problem of
human existence.

Erich Fromm

Love is not
consolation,
it is light.

Simone Weil

Everyone should
have the right to
say 'I love you'

What is done in love,
is well done.

Vincent van Gogh

The world is in need of
those whose life is one
burning love, selfless.

Swami Vivekananda

Love in all eight
tones and all five
semitones of the
world's full octave.

Stephen Fry

You, yourself, as much
as anybody in the
universe, deserve your
love and affection.

Buddha

Peace of mind comes when
your life is in harmony
with true principles and
values in no other way.

Stephen R. Covey

You see things;
and you say, 'Why?'
But I dream things
that never were; and
I say, 'Why not?'

George Bernard Shaw

I had simply never
found someone so right.
Sometimes this shocked
me so much that I was
unable to speak.

Ali Smith

Love isn't something you find. Love is something that finds you.

Loretta Young

Let the lover be disgraceful,
crazy, absent-minded.
Someone sober will worry
about events going badly.
Let the lover be.

Rumi

Love and compassion
are necessities, not
luxuries. Without them
humanity cannot survive.

Dalai Lama

Love is the best thing in
the world, and the thing
that lives the longest.

Henry Van Dyke

Sometimes the heart
sees what is invisible
to the eye.

H. Jackson Brown Jr

People think love is an emotion. Love is good sense.

Ken Kesey

Love with
every fibre of
your being!

No road is long with good company.

Turkish proverb

Love is the triumph
of imagination over
intelligence.

H. L. Mencken

In every living thing there
is the desire for love.

D. H. Lawrence

Wherever you go,
go with all your heart.

Confucius

Each moment of a lover's
hour is worth an age of
dull and common life.

Aphra Behn

Let love steal in
disguised as friendship.

Ovid

I see you everywhere, in
the stars, in the river; to me
you're everything that exists;
the reality of everything.

Virginia Woolf

Only do what your
heart tells you.

Diana, Princess of Wales

Kisses, even to the
air, are beautiful.

Drew Barrymore

Unless you love someone,
nothing else makes sense.

E. E. Cummings

Yes, there were two of us, but we were one.

Jeanette Winterson

Love will find a way
through paths where
wolves fear to prey.

Lord Byron

Because of a
great love, one is
courageous.

Lao Tzu

It doesn't matter who
you are or what you
look like so long as
somebody loves you.

Roald Dahl

Love makes
the world a
better place

Love loves to
love love.

James Joyce

I fell in love the way
you fall asleep: slowly,
and then all at once.

John Green

Ultimately love is
everything.

M. Scott Peck

Where there is love
there is life.

Mahatma Gandhi

Do all things
with love.

Og Mandino

To love and be
loved is to feel the
sun from both sides.

David Viscott

In order to be happy
oneself it is necessary
to make at least one
other person happy.

Theodor Reik

They slipped briskly
into an intimacy from
which they never
recovered.

F. Scott Fitzgerald

The greatest happiness of
life is the conviction that
we are loved; loved for
ourselves, or rather, loved
in spite of ourselves.

Victor Hugo

All, everything that
I understand, I only
understand because
I love.

Leo Tolstoy

Once you truly believe
you're worthy of love, you
will never settle for anyone's
second-best treatment.

Charles J. Orlando

Love comforteth like
sunshine after rain.

William Shakespeare

If a thing loves,
it is infinite.

William Blake

The best and most beautiful
things in the world cannot
be seen or even touched.
They must be felt with
the heart.

Helen Keller

It matters not who you love… or how you love, it matters only that you love.

John Lennon

If you're interested in finding out more about our books, find us on Facebook at **Summersdale Publishers** and follow us on Twitter at **@Summersdale**.

www.summersdale.com